# A
# DANGEROUS KNOWING

## four black
## women poets

**Barbara Burford**
**Gabriela Pearse**
**Grace Nichols**
**Jackie Kay**

**Sheba Feminist Publishers**

The following poems by Grace Nichols first appeared
in *i is a long memoried woman* and are reprinted
here by kind permission of *Karnak House*: 'We The
Women', 'Up My Spine', 'Like Clamouring Ghosts',
'Nimbus', 'I Coming Back', 'Night Is Her Robe', 'Love
Act', 'Wind A Change', 'Omen'.

First published by Sheba Feminist Publishers,
488 Kingsland Road. London E.8
Copyright © the collection, Sheba Feminist Publishers
Copyright © individual poems, the poets

Second Impression 1985.

British Library Cataloguing in Publication Data
A Dangerous Knowing
      1. English poetry — Women authors
      2. English poetry — Black authors
      I. Burford, Barbara
      821'914' 0803520396 PR1177
      ISBN 0-90719-28-2

Cover and Design by Shaheen Haq

Typeset in Century 10/11 by Lithoprint on 01-359-8288
Printed and bound by A. Wheaton and Co. Ltd, Exeter

# Contents

◆◆◆◆◆◆◆◆◆◆◆◆◆◆◆◆◆◆◆◆◆◆◆◆◆◆◆◆◆◆◆◆◆◆◆◆◆

◆◆◆◆◆◆◆◆◆◆◆◆◆◆◆◆◆◆◆◆◆◆◆◆◆◆◆◆◆◆◆◆◆◆◆◆

# Introduction

◆◆◆◆◆◆◆◆◆◆◆◆◆◆◆◆◆◆◆◆◆◆◆◆◆◆◆◆◆◆◆◆◆◆◆◆◆◆◆◆◆◆◆◆

> 'The furthest horizons of our hopes and fears are
> cobbled by our poems, carved from the rock ex-
> periences of our daily lives.
>
> **Audre Lorde,** *Sister Outsider*

Indeed it is these daily experiences, as much as the visions
and imaginations of Black women, which form the
substance of the poems you are about to read.

'*A Dangerous Knowing* marks a unique and historic moment in feminist publishing. Here, for the first time in
Britain, poetry written by four British based Black women is
brought together.

Black women have been writing poetry for centuries but
their words have often stayed within themselves; Black
women as poets and writers have remained invisible. Racism
in the publishing industry has ensured this invisibility by ig-
noring Black women's creativity and denying them access to
publishing, so many Black women have been reluctant to
name themselves as poets. It is with courage that the four
women in this book have taken this risk.

If poetry is an intense form of communication, creating
new ways of seeing through imaginative uses of language,
then these poets do that and more. Their ways of seeing
reach out and touch all Black women's lives, for we can see
our lives manifested in these words. These poets help create
new images of Black women and strengthen and encourage
their Black sisters to write.

Long overdue, *A Dangerous Knowing* reflects the variety
and depth of Black women's experiences. These poems
leave us with a sense of the complexities of Black women's
lives, sharing not only their fears, angers and sense of isola-
tion with us, but also their hopes, joys, laughter, and the
sensuality of being Black women. It is a vision of Black
women's lives which confirms their uniqueness. With it
goes a powerful presence: the spirit of resistence to soul-
destroying experiences.

Each poet has her own distinctive style yet the ability to
move and sharpen our senses is common to all four. Barbara

Burford's poem from which the title of this book comes, immediately alerts us to the creative force within women, as she says;

> *'Woman*
> *guard well your mystery*
> *Your own creative fruitfullness.*
> *It is a bloody, an ancient*
> *and a dangerous knowing.*

Barbara's poems are full of subtle nuances of ironic humour and affirmative joy.

The creative gift of which she speaks is shared by all four poets and confirmed in their work.

A sense of wry but optimistic humour is evident in Gabriela Pearse's poems which reflect her personal discovery of strength and identity;

> *'I want...*
> *To confront my fears,*
> *To dive long and deep*
> *in mother sea*
> *draw strength and love.*
> *To whom it my concern –*
> *I'm proud'*

The search for the roots of identity also feature strongly in many of Grace Nichol's poems. She forcefully conveys her rootedness in the experiences of her foremothers (a resistence and strength of will to survive) as in the poem 'We The Women':

> *'We the women making*
> *Something from this*
> *Ache-and-pain-a-me*
> *back-o-hardness'*

While the spirits of her foremothers inspire many of the poems which acknowledge her collective memories, she is also alert to the struggles of women today. Her poem 'Twentieth Century Witch Hunt', for instance, was written as a tribute to the women of Greenham Common who have been resisting the siting of nuclear missiles there.

Concern with pertinent issues of today is also reflected in Jackie Kay's poems. These have the capacity to make us look again and question accepted assumptions and understandings. 'We are all not sisters under the same moon' is a powerful challenge to a sisterhood conveniently assumed without any regard to our differences. Her moving account of the death of her close friend in 'And I still cannot believe it' makes us feel and share the loss too, a loss many of us can identify with: 'leaving me numb and terrified at another Black woman not surviving.'

The poems in this anthology expand our mental and emotional bounderies taking us through a variety of experiences: racism; the threat of nuclear holocaust; the joys of love between women as friends, lovers, mothers and sisters.

This collection of poems is a celebration of Black women's creative gifts – their 'dangerous knowing'.

*Pratibha Parmar*
*Sona Osman*

# Barbara

# Burford

## Barbara Burford

I am a thirty-nine-year-old Black woman, an active feminist and the mother of a ten-year-old daughter. I am committed to my work in medical research. Both my writing and my work go some way towards satisfying my deep curiosity. I write science fiction, poetry, and prose and can never win at Scrabble because I get drunk on words! I am presently writing a play 'Patterns' which is due to open this autumn in London. It was commissioned by *Changing Women's Theatre.*

# Women Talking

There are no parallels:
No lines – experiences,
carefully equidistant,
but never touching.

But, oh, there are resonances,
concerted leaps in the blood,
where we meet. Minor chords
modulating triumphantly to major.

These sequences:
Jewels scattered across
the dark fabric of our lives,
interweaving, complementing.

Eagle and air,
dolphin and sea,
make our waking   reality
a desired, though sharp-edged state.

For there are no parallels.
Just you and I
and our pasts, streaming forward
over our heads.

And we are mistresses
of strong, wild air,
leapers and sounders
of depths and barriers.

# Untitled

Woman
guard well your mystery:
Your own creative fruitfullness.
It is a bloody, an ancient,
and a dangerous knowing.
Beset with chimeras.
But it is the design
drawn on your bones;
the song hidden under your tongue;
the landscape painted
on the inside of your skin.

# In My Gift

I am, but had not
realised till now,
the love I have for you.
I cannot give it to you.
All gifts, all acts,
are like the sun
viewed through smoked glass.

I am dancing before you:
Hair flowing four miles
down the wind:
and asking:
'Will you take sugar?'

I am singing:
Oh miraculous concordance!
A thousand *a capella* hosannas;
and taking your arm
to cross the road.

I am flying:
Windhover and air,
melded, mated.
Watching the universe
revolve around you;
and leaning down,
to kiss, to be.

# State of the Art

Are you alone?
I am.
I tiptoe through crowds,
slide from encounters.
Alone.

I'm looking.
I don't have time for you.
No time for meaningless social drivel.
I might miss her,
the perfect mirror.

I'll know.
Oh, yes I will.
No question. I'll be bigger,
stronger, stripier.
Then I'll know.

Down offa my perch.
Runnin' on all fours,
a rose between my teeth.
Down — Looky here!

Then I'll ride my bike backwards.
Then I'll use mouthwash.
Eat red kidney beans,
dress on sundays.

Hey! Am I boring you?
Why are you sliding away?
I'm strangely prepared to talk to you.
Not communicate — ya understand.
Just practising my art.
Hey — !

# The Nth Day of Christmas

My dear,
I wish you a Busby Berkeley hell
of strictly choreographed thighs;
metronome smiles, and crotches
in relentless three-four time.

Oh, may you drown in ostrich feathers.
Strangle on sequins,
OD on dimpled whimsy.
And all this before
fifty-two matched white pianos
fall on you.

Not entering into the spirit?
Losing my sense of frivolity?
Bitter, twisted and frustrated?
Damn Right!

# Introspection Blues

There is a humour
that turns each slight,
each rejection;
into the self-loathing
that makes perverts
of all who dare approach.

There is the kind of heart
that mews cowardly,
at every wind-change of opinion.
gyroscopic at each of misery's
cardinal points.
Constant in inconstancy.

There is a kindliness
more deadly than hate.
lifting each painfully
healed scab.
Spreading a stinging ointment
of charm.
Raising consciousness, heartening,
those long gratefully numb.

There is a gift.
blessed with empathic amnesia.
The suddenly narrowed eyes
in the joker's face.
that sees the many
tiny deaths.
The touch, light upon
the newly sutured soul.

There is a dance.
feet in the mire,
arms vain in the wind,
eyes fixed on the stars.
And there is a rainbow rope,
woven by a million aspirations
today alone.
Here, I'll sing you a strand,
If you will live me the fibre.

# Sisterwrite

See me walking down
Upper Street:
Windy winter sunlight
pouring, hissing, through
impassive me. But inside
every step, a thousand
sparkling arabesques.
Every swing of the arms
a buck and wing.
Snap   Stonefaced.
I've done it.
Persephone has bought
two glowing ears of wheat
to take down into the
marital hades.
Just two thin iconaclastic
books of verse.
But now, Persephone knows
where the cornucopia lives.
She no longer eats from
Pluto's hand.
Is she getting ready to
bite it?

# In Solitary

See me:
Left foot forward, fingers in a magic ward.
Out across the abyss.
Line drawn, chip balanced.
Expelled from dark paradise.
No thought of return – 'tis a sin.
The bottle. No more the wine.
Once fruit. Now forever husk.

Watch me:
Dormant till my bloody flowering.
Pulsing with an ancient rhythm.
Moon, not sun.
Birth and death. Spring and winter.
Beguiling, strident.
Sowing the seeds of my own enslavement.
Weaving each afresh the tangelfoot net –
Love.
Buy one, use one.
The disposable, pull-up gender.
Oh, so soft. Such pretty colours.
Multifaceted, mirrored receptacles.

But what if I say:
I will be neither wine, nor flagon.
What if I sidestep your hasty pavanne.
Let none gainsay the heady lunar rushes.
Be clumsy, be irate.
Be twice thirteen and thirteen,
and no longer desperate.
Dance along the walls of my prison.

Snap my fingers:
Create a sun.
Squat, and in travail,
give birth to my own world.
Beat out new tempos on my flabby thighs.
Make windbells of my heart, and
glad flutes of my bones.
Whisper to myself songs of strange beguilement.

Then cross my line:
Pick up my gauntlet. If you can.
For I will not let down the drawbridge
of my bony castle.
I and my fancies safe remain.
We refuse your abyss, and your rope.
Cannot see your net.
Your cloudy reality,
We tread by our own heedless path.

# Christine

She was fine till april,
my child in my belly.
First a little mouse-breath
flutter in a body
that still resented her creation.
Then by christmas, love
that slept with
both hands clasped over her
pushes and swirlings.

To the country, to the nuns.
You're going to keep the child,
my dear?
How brave, but perhaps
you'll change your mind.

I hate azaleas, for
as they bloomed, my child faded
within my belly.
Till she was a dead steel ball
inside a walking wild coffin.
And no help.
Not even from her mother
who could not look.
Who listened to love clang
in a kidney-dish with
tight shut eyes.
And asked – What is it?

Providence, said the nuns,
kind providence.
A little girl.
And I don't even know
where she is buried.
Christine,
I hate azaleas.

# Daughters of Eve

Out of the flame-tipped
whisper-shadows beneath
The Tree of Life, I step.
Never to return.
Coiling, drifting down,
I stroke sister earth.
Ship to my life-raft,
both stretched and scarred
by birth wounds.

Swirling, shouting up,
a jewel dance in the air
at the corner of your vision,
I breathe your clouds,
cry you rain.
My grey lightening mane
lashes the blue scoured noon,
a diamond scatter of hail
flung from one hand,
a fine sugar-sift largesse
of snow, from the other.

Out of the flame-tipped
whisper-shadows beneath
The Tree of Life,
I have stepped.
I will never go back.
Mysterious keeper of the deep magics,
or heedless dragonfly
skim-dancing with time's river.
Out. Aware. Woman.

# The Other

For you are the dervish in my valley.
Flying out your hushing skirts encompass
the windsong of wheat and barley.
Your dusty bare feet
stamp out the poppy'd ditches.
Heel toe, arms spread,
clothed in mist or sunstream,
the cadence of my days.

For you are the salmon leaper
in my headlong flood. Stretching, flashing.
The deep undershimmer of my still riverbottom.
The smooth pebble
cool in my desert mouth.

For you are the secret
caverns in my slumbrous mountain chain.
The cloud shadows,
the falcon's killing stoop along my slopes.
My creaking glaciered scour to the sea.
My clay stopped, hoarded fountaining.

For you are the flame
on my hour candle.
My rhythms, circadian, lunar,
all resolve in your counterbeat.
The green unfolding,
the flamboyant flowering,
in my seasons' turning.
The reaper at my pained harvest,
the sower at my rebirth.

# Fallow Time

My perceptions change,
stripped bare by the wind
of reality.
Like the fraillest branchings
of the bare trees,
I am open, naked, exposed.
Come play me like the wind.
Bless me like the frail winter sun.
Clothe me in rich time
with translucent feathery green.
Then we will sing a whole
new song together:
Sister wind, sister tree.
Catching, holding, echoing.
A whole song.

# Gabriela

# Pearse

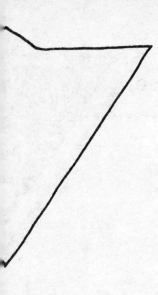

NINA PRESCOD

## Gabriela Pearse

I was born in Bogota Columbia twenty-two years ago of a
Trinidadian mother and English father and was raised in South
America, the Caribbean and England. I feel intensely multi-
cultural. I have a passion for people, their faces, bodies,
expressions and conversations, for dancing, talking and hugging.
I studied at Warwick University, evolved into a committed
feminist and am working through the hundreds of contradictions
that arise daily out of being a Black/Third World feminist
committed to social change personally, nationally and
internationally.

# Queiro — (I want/love)

I want
to hug and squeeze
myself.
And pull
off the stiff mask
and sweat of fear.

I want
a newness
I want to be it all
to myself
discover a shell
listen to the voice
of my dad.

Get beyond the patriarchy
beyond the lies
and love the witches
and love the 'tarts'.

And I want
to learn to
dissipate myself
spread over friends
and lovers and a room of my own.

I want to go to
the sea and play
laugh and cry
my ice-cream
falls fatally to sand
and there'll never be
another like it.

To confront my fears,
to dive long and deep
in mother sea
draw strength and love.
And paint my face
To Whom It May Concern —
I'm Proud!

# Mother

Mother duty instinct
Mother known and present –
in every judgement
in many lines I see her
I feel her weight
I love her.
Biting bear of scorn
you are
soft fine hairs on face
temple blue beats loud
and skips tense.
Smell skin black and cool
opening and closing up
your insecurity – yet so strong
a fine woman.
Unacknowledged face
mirror frowned in/on.
Small, inaccessible clouded over, stormy.
Vague wide voice
as you look up from the paper
stockings at ankles shoes on sides.
Real curiosity and pride looking at
what you produced.
Listening from a different culture
looking on uncertain, disapproving,
unrecognising. I see the me of your eyes,
Wanting me to take flight?
but watching the kite.
So wise, so wise
and watching, so protective.

# St. Helens, and St. Catherines school for girls

Into you green beehive,
unwittingly, I walked.
Decorus inspection of the new species.
Acceptance impossible, but;
My shade not stridently offensive,
my features not uncomfortably 'native',
in accents of digresion, disinfection
proclaimed me Honorary White.
Invitation to you; condensed milk?
Charmingly caged, occasionally
obliging with unusual noise.
Once the simplicity was shattered
by a red tear shed at your numbed senses.
and the raised eyebrow paused,
before the tepid tea, wondered me,
if you were soggy paper after all.

# Autobiography.

In my womb
a – warm
a sucked thumb,
enclosed, I turn to
watch my path
umbilically spiralling
behind me – leading
precisely to this moment
                    this history
                    this time.
The Columbian tombed
God-father-priest
armed – killed,
watches clove and cinnamon
salsa.

I am this
sixties history
from my cot.

In my world
I watch the
black and white
            quiver in love
                        in hate
                        insane
I am to be the brown bridge
that builds
a trust.

My black my white
dissolve.
A third language later
I come in to the cold
from calypso warmth
to learn.

Tumbled around classes
I contort to become
Sound-
ing
black
and white
and red.

In my space
mirrored
my face.
watch it slowly
cocooning out ...
recognising its sex
rediscovering
creating
spawning
strength – in division
in
wimmin loving wimmin loving
life
the black
the white
the smiling birth.

# Wedding Guest

It is with your throat
my voice
dares to
spit obscenities.
Your hands arrogance
handle ...

Proper sentiment
of juries
watching how
you will eel
yourself out of his
blessed hands
hands consecrated
Pope's mandate
to grope.

Their eyes tear you
for a sign of
enjoyment, Ready
to pounce beady
bullets into newly
acclaimed whore.

And firewater
all the better allows them to
kiss your hand.
Sweet mango kiss
in the morning
begging your pardon
using your son's innocent
3 year old eyes,
to bring the waves of guilt
tidal or gently lapping
into a heart already humiliated.

Perhaps the thoughts in
the restless bed
were too harsh ...
after-all ...

Caterpillers when they
know not what they do
and are blessed when
their wings expand
into proud colourful, beautiful ...

Bless me father for I ...
Father, where were
you that night?
Where was the
baby smile
you used to
bounce what
was yours
on paternal
oh so paternal
knee?
Where was your wife
your 'life'
lilly white
portrate smile
to her glowing
where are you now?
You confuse
bemuse
amuse me.
Turn hatred into pity
then white fury.

What goes on in your penis?

# Soft evening blues

Tomorrow – you go to see

your sweet-perfumed-delicate-sexed-girlfriend

And I watch, I watch candle shaped faces melt
And listen, listen to Indian tales and missile crisis
And taste, taste the post study sweet digestive lingering

I feel solid and black and red
I feel compassionate and human
Full breasted, heavy sexed
I feel concentrated complicated powerful
Clean and Wise

And – flash of a sudden in an instant glow;
contented and happy with myself ...
                    yea down to me moustache!

# Credo

I will home
Only enveloped
with sisters
aunts cuddles
and comrades.

Alone you want
me, naked
you want me
snaked and sexy
you want me.

You want comfort
filled arms
not the fight
in me
is me
to you right
who are enough.

I will home
only alone
with confidence
with stature
with out gift
of casserole smiled.

I will home
uncringing pushed
off the brink
loving my body
guilt hangs up by
door – shapeless
naming the nameless
fears – proud

I will come home.

Feminism gradually becomes painful but ...

# Turning back is
# no longer possible.

◆◆◆◆◆◆◆◆◆◆◆◆◆◆◆◆◆◆◆◆◆◆◆◆◆◆◆◆◆◆◆◆◆◆◆◆◆◆◆◆◆◆◆

Mother you don't belong here
you are my source
your spring has been diverted.
For another years learning
takes me into dangerous waters.

The sharks are out
teeth – to isolate,
cruising in many guises
grinning their 'common sense'
as you try your luck
crossing the line.

Snip snap makes you
off-the-edge
over-the-top:
Freak.

Cutting edge ventures,
but into an uncommon language
a new pair of specs
which distorts the normal
to who/ to which/ to wooo ... Twit.
Owl like observations
seeing in darkness
blind to christian light.

The Truth ...
I tried to phone him
– objectively –
he'd pissed off centuries ago
with the inquisition.

Yet the old vultures remain
presiding, perched, limp,
and vicious.
Controlling distorting all
to gracious safe
white male normality.

# Alice

You,
    are milky intrepid.

You,
    are soft as marshmellow inside.

My pulse syncronises
halted palm stopped
at distance –
    ... and waved on to lap
      at your shore.

Dog wanting to
curl in brown thighs.

You,
    I want
    to savage
    to find the heart
    in one swoop
    not wait for years
    to trickle it through.

You,
    invite me into
    your open house
    worthless for all
    guests are not like
    me yet valued.

I dream to be
against the grain
the 'One'.

Words solidify
around you
cringe at themselves
change pink floss
to red brick,
      and clash.

# Hot Summer

Minds bent daily
by warped mirrors.
Cancerous leaves
hair falls out
from the autumn of our age.
The silences
the lies were ears,
to tape and take away.
Where we are, our roots
need water
yet fish we eat gives
limbless listless children
twenty years on.
On and up forever
to house the rats
so that the cats
can pounce on regulated
exits if it gets too hot.
In Brixton the order
in Brixton the law
broke down down down ...

In the minds of the
masses the media
God's truth lives on and on.
'Common petty thieves
out for what they could get'
This summer, after white
'terrorists' starve themselves for life,
     and black kids stone themselves for pride,
         my mother turns slowly mad.

# Grenada ... Heathrow ... London

Sun dance
sun dial
around
the cloister
of a distance
too great.

A culture
a class
away
a warmth
a world
away.

Half smile
ginger cat
sneeks
across face
across place
of longing.

Silence filled
with words
with each
with you.

Unknowing
unsure
unnerving
a laugh
echoes.

Trip wire
around
barbed comment
keeps you
off balance.

◆◆◆◆◆◆◆◆◆◆◆◆◆◆◆◆◆◆◆◆◆◆◆◆◆◆◆◆◆◆◆◆◆◆◆◆◆◆◆◆◆◆◆◆◆◆◆◆◆◆◆◆

Wanting home
enveloping
in cotton wool
the ache and need.

The dampened dance of time will take its toll.

# Grace

# Nichols

DAVID CUTTING

## Grace Nichols

Born 1950 in Guyana where she grew up and worked among other things as pupil teacher, reporter and free-lance writer. She came to Britain in 1977 and has had poems published in journals and magazines such as *Frontline, Ambit, Kunapipi, Poetry Review, Artrage, City Limits, Third Eye*. She has done many readings over the last two years including appearances at the Poetry Olympics, Angels of Fire Festival and Poetry Society and readings for BBC, Australian and German Radio.

Her Cycle of poems '*I is a long memoried Woman*' won the 1983 Commonwealth Poetry Prize (Published by *Karnac House*, a small Caribbean publishing house). She is also the author of two children's books 'Trust You Wriggly' a collection of stories published by *Hodder & Stoughton* and 'Baby Fish and other Stories' a collection of folk stories which she published herself with illustrations by her ten-year-old daughter.

*Virago* is bringing out another collection of her poems '*The Fat Black Woman's Poems*' in September this year (1984) and *Hodder and Stoughton* has brought out another children's book, set in London, 'Leslyn in London.'

Some of her poems appear in 'News for Babylon', the recently published West Indian British anthology (*Chatto & Windus*). Grace Nichols also writes poems for children and some of these appear in the *Cambridge* children's anthology, 'I Like That Stuff.'

# We the Women

We the women who toil
unadorn
heads tie with cheap
cotton

We the women who cut
clear fetch dig sing

We the women making
something from this
ache-and-pain-a-me
back-o-hardness

Yet we the women
who praises go unsung
who voices go unheard
who deaths they sweep
aside
as easy as dead leaves

# Up my Spine

I see the old dry-head woman
leaning on her hoe
twist-up and shaky like a cripple insect

I see her ravaged skin
the stripes of mold
where the whip fall hard

I see her missing toe
her jut-out hipbone
from way back time when she had a fall

I see the old dry-head woman
leaning on her hoe
twist-up and shaky like a cripple insect

I see the pit of her eye

I hear her rattle bone laugh
putting a chill up my spine

# Like Clamouring Ghosts

Last night I dream a terrible
dream
I dream about the Gods forcing
me to drink blood from my father
skull
forcing me to eat dirt

And when I try to run the chiefs
and elders of the tribe come after
me like clamouring ghosts

In this dream I see my own face
wild and greyish with terror

What hope have I if the old ones
turn against me in my dreams

# Nimbus

Sitting in the shadows
countering darkness/
with darkness
fingers caught
in the rhythmic
braiding of her
hair

room infused with
lavender
and the nimbus
growing from herself

Listen
hear her laughter
soft and harsh
in the darkness

# Omen

I require an omen, a signal
I kyan not work this craft
on my own strength

alligator teeth
and feathers
old root and powder

I kyan not work this craft
this magic black
on my own strength

Dahomey lurking in my shadows
Yoruba lurking in my shadows
Ashanti lurking in my shadows

I am confused
a lust for guidance
a signal, a small omen
perhaps a bird picking
at my roof

# I Coming Back

I coming back Massa
I coming back

mistress of the underworld
I coming back

colour and shape
of all that is.evil
I coming back

dog howling outside
yuh window
I coming back

ball-a-fire
and skinless higue
I coming back

hiss in yuh ear
and prick in yuh skin
I coming back

bone in yuh throat
and laugh in yuh skull
I coming back

I coming back Massa
I coming back

# Night is Her Robe

Night is her robe
Moon is her element

Quivering and alert
she's stepping out behind
the fields of sugarcane

She's stepping out softly
she's stepping out carefully
she's bending/she's stalking
she's flitting/she's crawling

Quivering and alert
she's coming to the edge
of her island forest

Now with all the care
of a herbalist
she's gathering strange weeds
wild root
leaves with the property
both to harm and to heal

Quivering and alert
Quivering and alert
She's leaving the edge
of her island forest

# Love-Act

She enter into his Great House
her see-far looking eyes
unassuming

He fix her with his glassy stare
and feel the thin fire in his blood
awakening

Soon she is the fuel
that keep them all going

He/his mistresswife
and his children who take
to her breasts like leeches

He want to tower above her
want her to raise her ebony
haunches and when she does
he think she can be trusted
and drinks her in

And his mistresswife
spending her days in rings
of vacant smiling
is glad to be rid of the loveact

But time passes

Her sorcery
cut them like a whip

She hide her triumph
and slowly stir the hate
of poison in.

# Wind a Change

Wind a change
blow soft but
steadfast

ripple the spears
of sugar cane
stir slow the leaves
of indigo

Dance
waltz
soothe
this old mud-wattle
hut
bring if you can
the smell of Dahomey
again

Wind a change
cool mountain water
open river flower

But pass easy
up the big house
way
let them sleep
they happy white sleep

Yes, Wind a change
keep yuh coming fire
secret

# Between Women

We recognise each other
exhilarate in the recognition
of each other
across the kitchen table
we spend hours
reclaiming
obscured from history our mothers
talk about our fondness
for our wombs and lovers

Disappoint
we disappoint each other
use and betray
use and betray each other
sometimes we even choose
to kill each other

But the need to fill
the pages of silence between us
remain

# Twentieth Century
# Witch Chant

◆◆◆◆◆◆◆◆◆◆◆◆◆◆◆◆◆◆◆◆◆◆◆◆◆◆◆◆◆◆◆◆◆◆◆◆◆◆◆◆◆◆◆

Resurrect the ashes of the women burnt as witches
resurrect the ashes/mould the cinders
stir the cauldron/resurrect those witches

Resurrect the pieces of the women gone as priestesses
resurrect the pieces/restitch/rebone/reheal
the fingers' secrets/resurrect those priestesses

Resurrect the voices of the women gone as prophetesses
resurrect the voices/respeech the tongues
intone the sounds/resurrect those prophetesses

Resurrect those witches
return their things to spell with

Resurrect those priestesses
return their robes to gown with

Resurrect those prophetesses
return their eyes to socket with

Resurrect
Resurrect
Resurrect

As for the boys playing with their power toys
entoad them all

# Of course when they ask for poems about the 'Realities' of black women

what they really want
at times
is a specimen
whose heart is in the dust

a mother-of-sufferer
trampled/oppressed
they want a little black blood
undressed
and validation
for the abused stereotype
already in their heads

or else they want
a perfect song

I say I can write
no poem big enough
to hold the essence

of a black woman
or a white woman
or a green woman

and there are black women
and black women
like a contrasting sky
of rainbow spectrum

touch a black woman
you mistake for a rock
and feel her melting
down to fudge
cradle a soft black woman
and burn fingers as you trace
revolution
beneath her woolly hair

and yes we cut bush
to clear paths
for our children
and yes we throw sprat
to catch whale
and yes
if need by we'll trade
a piece-a-pussy
that see the pickney dem
in the grip-a-hungry-belly

still there ain't no
easy belly category

          for a black woman
          or a white woman
          or a green woman

and there are black women
strong and eloquent
and focussed

and there are black women
who somehow always manage to end up
frail victim

and there are black women
considered so dangerous
in South Africa
they prison them away

                   maybe this poem is to say
that I like to see
we black women
full-of-we-selves walking

◆◆◆◆◆◆◆◆◆◆◆◆◆◆◆◆◆◆◆◆◆◆◆◆◆◆◆◆◆◆◆◆◆◆◆◆◆◆◆◆◆◆◆◆◆◆◆◆◆◆◆◆◆◆

          crushing out
          with each dancing step
the twisted self-negating
history
we've inherited

          crushing out
          with each dancing step

# Jackie

## Kay

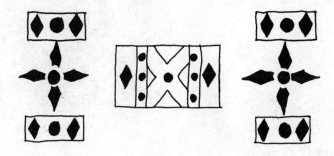

INGRID POLLARD

## Jackie Kay

I was born in 1961 and brought up in Scotland. I was raised on politics and demonstrations so I have always had, as far back as I can remember, a commitment to change. Writing is very important to me because it helps me to define what I want to change and why. Some of my poems have previously appeared in *Artrage* and *Feminist Review No. 17*. I have had a short story published in *Everyday Matters 2*. I like discovering surprises in people, reading and talking and talking, and talking ...

# So you think I'm a mule?

"Where do you come from?"
'I'm from Glasgow.'
"Glasgow?"
'Uh huh. Glasgow.'
The white face hesitates
the eyebrows raise
the mouth opens
then snaps shut
incredulous
yet too polite to say outright
liar
she tries another manoeuvre
"And your parents?"
'Glasgow and Fife.'
"Oh?"
'Yes. Oh.'
Snookered she wonders where she should go
from here –
"Ah, but you're not pure"
'Pure? Pure what.
Pure white? Ugh. What a plight
Pure? Sure I'm pure
I'm rare ...'
"Well, that's not exactly what I mean,
I mean ... you're a mulatto, just look at ...'
'Listen. My original father was Nigerian
to help with your confusion
But hold on right there
If you Dare mutter mulatto
hover around hybrid
hobble on half-caste
and intellectualize on the
"mixed race problem",
I have to tell you:
take your beady eyes offa my skin;
don't concern yourself with
the "dialectics of mixtures";
don't pull that strange blood crap

on me Great White Mother.
Say, I'm no mating of a
she-ass and a stallion
no half of this and half of that
to put it plainly  purely
I am Black
My blood flows evenly, powerfully
and when they shout "Nigger"
and you shout "Shame"
ain't nobody debating my blackness.
You see that fine African nose of mine,
my lips, my hair, You see lady
I'm not mixed up about it.
So take your questions, your interest,
your patronage. Run along.
Just leave me.
I'm going to my Black sisters
to women who nourish each other
on belonging
There's a lot of us
Black women struggling to define
just who we are
where we belong
and if we know no home
we know one thing:
we are Black
we're at home with that.'
"Well, that's all very well, but ..."
'I know it's very well.
No But. Good bye.'

# Tulips

My tulips are dying
petals curled back on
themselves
wrinkled at the tips
stems loose and bent
leaves olive coloured
they stoop in a carafe
in a pool of water
they have lost that tall
straight-backed elegance
erect and closed in
when they revealed nothing
of the stores inside
the black cones tiny
huddled close secrets.

# Happy ending

When I remember
the fairytales
read to me as treats
I remember
the scary bits
big bad wolf
three little piggies
squeaking in terror
what big teeth you've got
Mirror Mirror On the Wall
and they are all
mixed up. I chose
to forget
the pat happy endings:
the Prince's kiss
resting uncomforably
on my imagination,
my memory forces him
and his gallantry to
get lost in the woods
And I wished
out of wickedness
that Rapunzel had
short cropped hair.

Tonight
my imagination gallops
across moors wishing
she didn't have to conjure up
a happy ending
for another dyke
in yet another
misery-making
lesbian novel.

Maybe Rapunzel
gets rescued by a
woman firm of muscle
and strong of heart

who takes the scissors out
after dinner and says
'You could use a hair cut'
Or maybe the mirror
would reflect a dark woman
with shiny skin and nappy hair.
Sometimes I'd like to hear
a lesbian story where
the woman I'm following
does not die
in the end.

Somewhere
hanging tentatively
on the edge of our pain
there must be something
that edges close to happiness
and at least
enters into love
and splashes in those
fairytale words
demanding
some strength
out of this pain.

Sometimes
we will
ride on the crest
of that powerful pain
and ease each other
onto soft sand
our love
rounding the hard edges
of our downs
into ups.
Whilst we lie on
this solid bed
we make our own stories.

# We are not all sisters under the same moon

and the moon is never the same two nights
running into different shapes choosing
to light up a certain crescent or to be
full and almost round or to slide into
a slither tilted backwards looking up to the stars.

Before this night is over and before
this new dawn rises we have to see
these particular changes   speak to
our guarded uncertain before singing
Sisterhood is Powerful. Once we see
that light reflect our various colours;
when we feel complexity clear as an orange sun
moving into the morning maybe we can sit
here in the shade and talk
meeting each other's eyes with a sparkle
that is not afraid to see the lone bright poppy
the dying azalea – the rage in this summer evening;
nor afraid to question the dent
in the dream or the words missing
from the story.

When you see my tone
changes with the sun or ill health
when you realise
I  am  Not  a  Definition
perhaps we can move on.

For I am not only a strong woman
with a Scorpio rising I am
not about to dance with daffodils
everyday making putty out of my wishes
to shape my future needs. I have no
definite tomorrow only a longing that
I will write to pick out lights
that cast curious shadows in the dark.

And yes it would be easy to pat
the back of my confidence
smacking out my fears with assurance
saying strong women never hesitate:
looking inward into this particular
Black woman helps me look outward;
only by questioning the light
in my eyes can I refuse to be
dazzled by the lie in yours —
we are not all sisters
under the same moon.

# Dustbins and dreams

I'm going to
open that glass door
and listen to the moon whispering
solemn secrets of my sisters
and stare at the stars
gleaming proudly
twinkling after tears
and tell the wisps of the sky's curls
that I long for a soft pillow
to snuggle into
to soothe my soul
and dream warm dreams.
Not wistful. Just warm,
the kind of dreams that'll hug me tight,
the kind of company to keep in the night.

I'm going to
open that glass door
and be a buddy for
the night air. We will, oh we will
conspire together holding each others'
fog-damp hands, blending mellow mist
cool mellow mist to gulp down and swirl
in our bellies. And those bright
dazzling white glittering white
shamelessly white corridors
of tormenting trolleys and Largactil and Doctors
(whose too-tight trousers hug their balls)
Oh! they will be captured twirling
in their damp rank vapour.

I'm going to open that glass door
I said, open it wide
and holler holler to my neighbours:
'It's a disgrace! Their stench is
an offence to our streets, to our Black souls'
And a wee woman, who wears no wig
who is hugging her Blackness so tight,
will exclaim: 'Out rage ous Call the hygiene!'
And they'll arrive –
the women with the plastic bags –
and pack them and I'll perch
like a pigeon on my window sill
and watch that big van trundle
with their weight up the main street.

I'm going to throw open that glass door
and whistle to that ice cream cone cloud
to come down
and the two of us, just the two of us,
dark sisters lovers to lick and soothe
each others' souls, will sit quiet watching
stars play hopskotch with an old out of shape
tin can and I promise with my blood
that I'll tell you out-loud-ringing-loud
of my warm wrath that's still whirring
around inside, inside with my blood,
inside way down past my guts.
I'll tell you how I hate those white rays
and bright flashes how the sunlight
is a spy who is planning my fire.
And I'll laugh another iridescent tear
and that drop of my anguish will wet your soul
and you'll stretch out a warm-wet hand
and say: 'I'm here.'

# The sky changes every second now

Tonight I sit typing my poem for you
as the sky changes from cool blue
and the sun goes down
a luminous tangerine falling
into violets
the trees are huge and Black
once again
I am touching the power in me
that ancient Black Woman
waiting within
for me to call her
let her out to roam
about my hopes and fears
you are in my vision
the dark wise tree
you are with me Dida, always.

# Intensity

There's a time
when my whirling
plays squash
off the walls
in my head
and I'm whispering to myself
'have a break have a kitkat'
but I keep on
and on
battering
and I'm fed up with being like this
heavy's lover
and intensity's best friend
a real big demander
always wanting instant
instant cups of warmth
instant smiles
and squeezes
and never allowing space
for you right now
to knit and sniff
and be still with yourself.
I'm just dying to ask you
'What are you thinking?'

# And I still cannot believe it.

You were alive
alive
last night in my
dream so real so
like yourself your
cheeks high and shiny
strokes of pain sweeping
across them your head
with that unmistakable shape
held at an angle tilted towards
pride
and I saw you
I wanted you
again and again
I awoke this morning
crying for you
reaching out to hold you
desperate for movement
for time to stretch our possibilities
for hours to let a sprinkling
of our dreams take
root
time to talk
to speak out the
lumps in our throats
the unsaid heavy
weighing down the few
spoken words
whilst all that time
I was conscious somewhere
deep and hard
that you are now dead
dead a deliberate monotone
at the back of my head
dead
dead
you enter my dreams
at night

leaving me bitter in the
morning
leaving me astonished
at the crash the silence
that one cruel stroke
that obliterated your potential
leaving me numb and terrified
at another Black woman not
surviving
and I still cannot believe it.
and I still cannot believe it.

# Remi

Watching
my pain rise
uh huh
in flame oranges
hot fiery ball
piercing
through blue
and silver
in anger

Watching
my pain set
mm Hmm
sliding dully
down
slow motion
peaches
pale slither
into purples
in sadness

Remi? Are you still listening?
I'm frightened of unpeeling
those angry oranges
maybe they will
burst into fire
spitting segments on my tongue
burn me up
Remi  I dread tasting blood on my own reflection

Remi – are you there?
I sang to you before
my soul echoed a longing
        you returned
we held each other's need
and our sweat stuck
our bare Black skins together;
we tried to banish that image forever

Remi  I am calling your Black name
                    to rise up
        to stand up
                    to speak out
I am making
                    demands
by our graveside
bouncing on Black earth
        I want some of that
Black moisture back
just to roll my tongue around
to lick slowly

Remi
they image-murdered all of us
and this
is our insurrection
We Will Be Back
to claim it
isn't that right Remi?
We will be back

to reclaim our memories
            our moist tongues
    our songs
            our skin
                    our sweat
our blood

We will be back.
We will be back.
We will be back.